why men are like shoes

A woman's guide
to finding the
perfect ~~shoes~~ guy

KERRY HOWARD

Diva Publications

WHY MEN ARE LIKE SHOES
First published in Australia in 2018
by Diva Publications
a wholly owned subsidiary of
Ms Pink Enterprises Pty Ltd
10 Euroka Street
Narrabundah ACT 2604

National Library of Australia Cataloguing-in-Publication entry

Creator:	Howard, Kerry A., 1969-author
Title:	Why men are like shoes: a woman's guide to finding the right guy / Kerry Howard
ISBN:	9780995425101 : hard cover
Subjects:	Single Women—Life skills guides
	Women—conduct of life
	Self-actualization (Psychology) in women

Cover design by Designerability

www.kerryannhoward.com
www.mspinkherself.com

Dedication

For my daughters - Stephanie and Elysha

Steph – for being the lovely, supportive, understanding and fabulous individual that you have become.

Elysha – for being the wonderfully inspiring and unique person that you are. For inspiring me to create this analogy in the first place and for continually asking me following a 'date'...

"So Mum - what sort of shoes was he?"

The Dating Scene

For all of you lovely ladies who are 'Shoe Shopping', this book was created to explain the process of dating.

When you go shopping for that perfect pair you have to remember some simple rules:

1. You need to have a good understanding of what you have in your wardrobe so that you can find a pair that goes with everything

2. The first time you try them on you need to leave them in the shop, then go back and check them out again

3. Never 'Impulse Buy' – it's a sure fire way to find that your hard earned cash is wasted

4. If you really like them – put them on 'Lay-By'... That way you know that no one else will buy them, but you can still decide they are not really for you later on

5. When you commit to the purchase be sure you have taken all things into account, and remember that the ultimate test of the perfect fit is 'comfort'

The Blundstone Boot

This is a no nonsense, down to earth, practical 'good bloke'. This boy smells earthy, just soap and water for him.

Conversation is simple - sport (particularly football) with a bit of current affairs thrown in. He listens to the radio and has Slim Dusty records in the cupboard.

Dates are simple, the local pub for a counter meal. If you are craving romance, this man is not for you. However, he is stable, loyal and not afraid of hard work or commitment. Marriage – after all isn't that what we're meant to do?

No doubting the long term comfort of this boot... They are very versatile. They can be worn in the paddock for a bit of hard yakka, or you can add taps for some unique dancing shoes!

Anyone will tell you they need to be worn in very well. In the beginning, when new, they can be tight and uncomfortable, but long-term use softens the leather and makes them extremely comfortable!

However, don't be conned into thinking they can be worn with a dress or skirt – the look is all wrong.

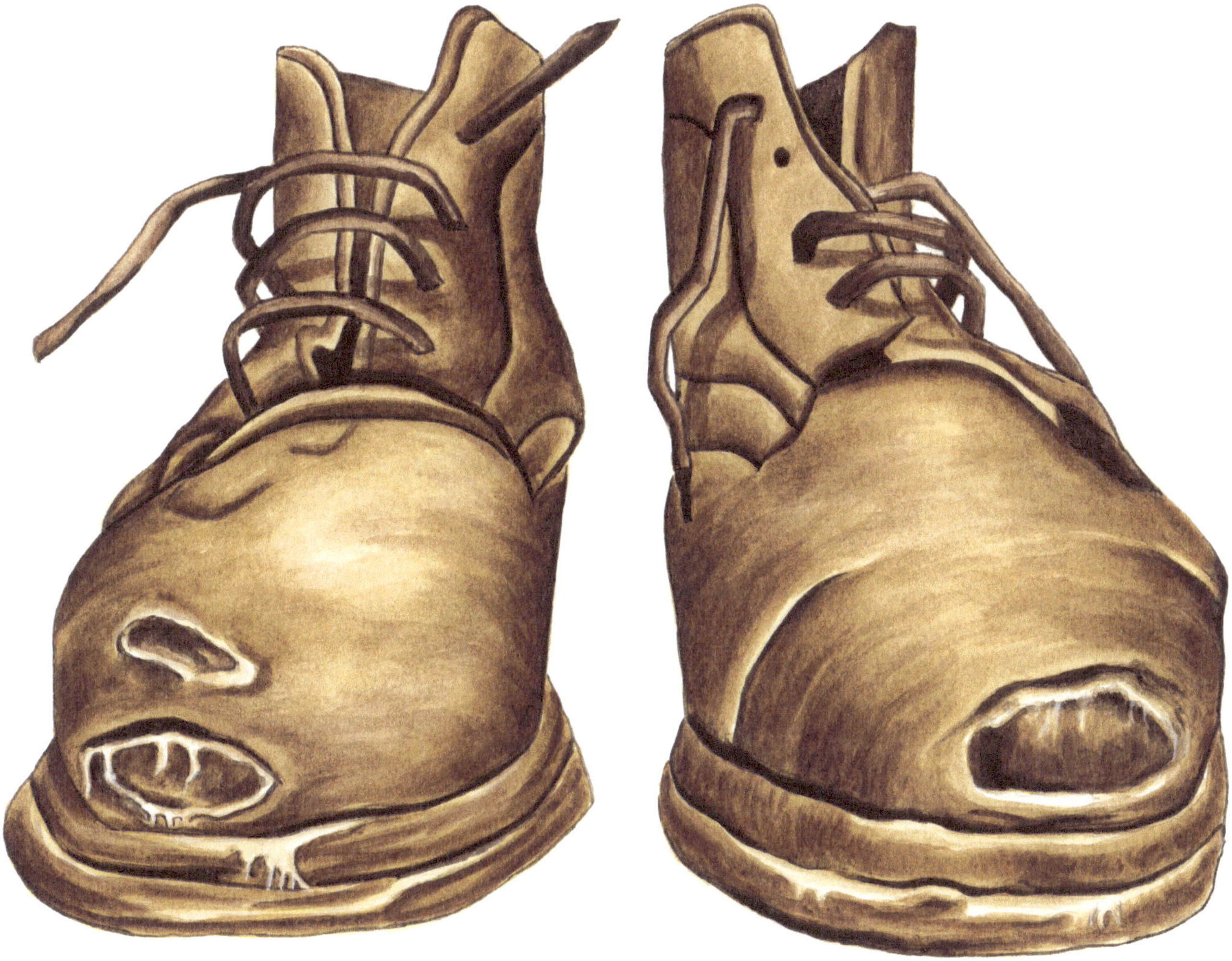

The Stiletto

This man presents himself with a sense of style. He is flashy, effusive and makes you feel like you're the only woman in the room. Be aware ladies – there are many women in the room and he has an eye for all of them!

That's not to say that he's unfaithful – necessarily. However, he likes women, he loves life and exudes sex appeal. He smells great, scrubs up alright and he knows it.

You need to be just as confident in yourself to be able to sustain a long-term relationship with the Stiletto!

Pretty cool to look at, these shoes make your legs look fabulous and your bum tight...

However, the height of the heels can cause pain when worn for extended periods of time, new ones always cause blisters... In the long term you will develop bunions.

Not the most versatile - they look great with an evening dress but they are no good for mowing the lawn!

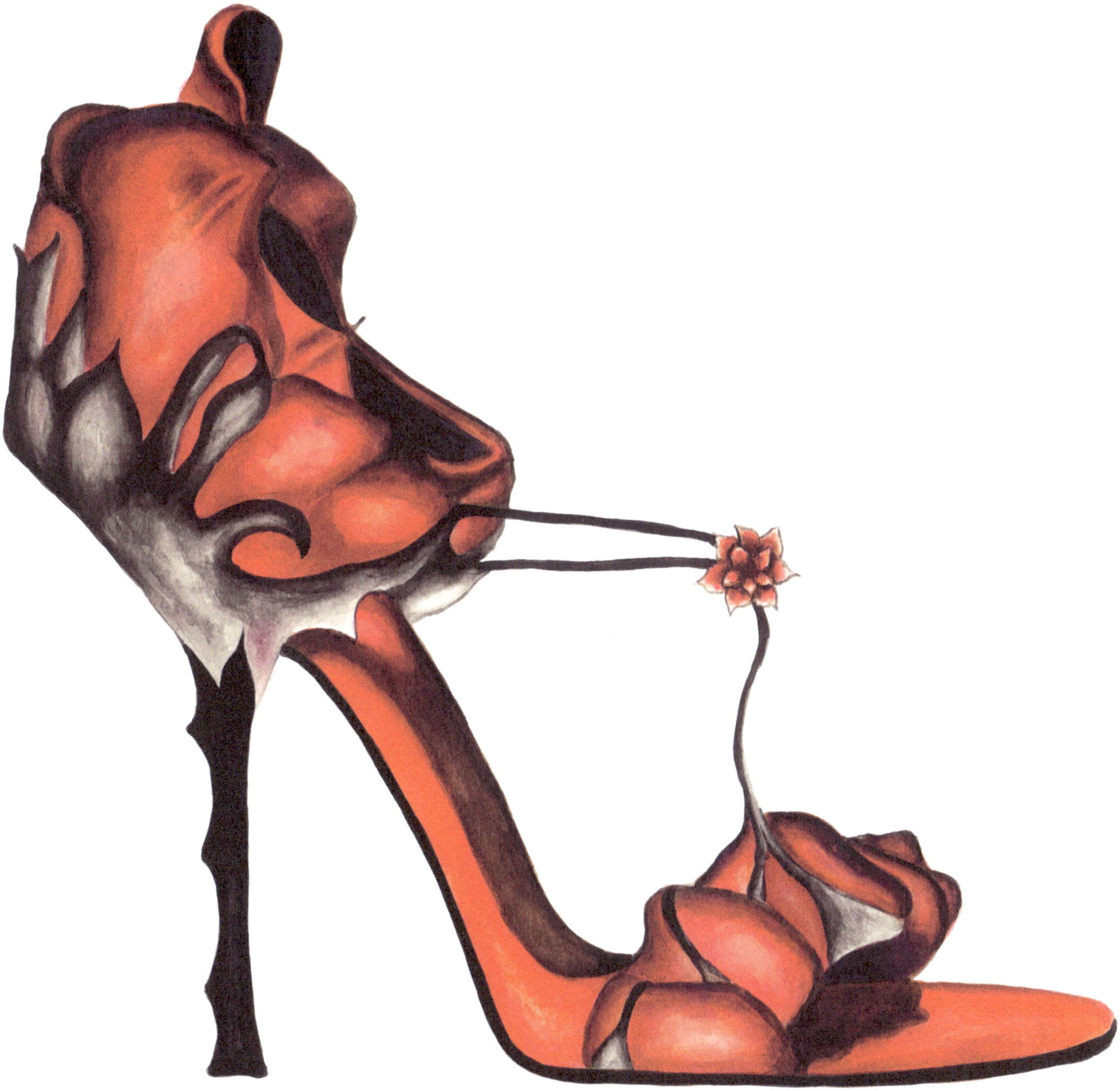

The Running Shoes

This guy is buff, looks good and carries himself with an air of confidence. He is very active, team oriented and he won't necessarily have much time for you.

If you are equally sporty, then your competitive natures may complement each other. Otherwise there is a great potential for disappointment.

He can be romantic when he needs to, but it's like a game – usually with a specific purpose or goal in mind! He may actively chase you, but when the chase is over and you're caught, you might find he tires of you very quickly... Game Over!

These shoes always appear comfortable from the first try. They seem to cushion your feet and are usually a snug fit – making you feel like they were made for you. However, don't forget that they are a purpose built shoe.

Comfortable initially, once purchased you may discover a small piece of leather or strapping that never softens and will always rub and cause angst.

When worn regularly they tend to wear out quickly. Honestly ladies, these only look good with your track pants!

The Italian Leather Boots

This man carries an air of sophistication but without arrogance. Usually reasonably well dressed, but not 'flamboyant'. He is quiet and studious, holds down a professional job and can engage in an intelligent conversation.

If you are looking for spark and excitement, this may not be the man for you! He may not excite you much – but he is loyal, committed and will ensure you have a comfortable life.

However, he is very BROWN! If stability is your yearning... Then this is the man for you.

A classic to look at, we've all got a pair in the wardrobe somewhere... They have a timeless quality about them, but that's because they never stand out.

They can be worn with almost anything – jeans and dresses. However, they are not evening wear.

Usually very comfortable, these will hang around for years and are often the ones we go back to when our must have boots of this season break a heel!

The Boat Shoe

This boy is relaxed... He likes the finer things in life and knows how to get them, but he is not 'pretentious' about it.

He'll take you to nice restaurants, probably order for you and match it perfectly with a nice wine. Don't expect any great overtures of 'love language' – this man is down to earth, but focused!

He expects you to reflect him, to be presentable – not the focus of attention. Don't outshine him, he is the achiever in the relationship.

Like a 'Toorak Tractor' they have a slightly classy feel to them – so they often end up being the shoes you choose for a casual weekend BBQ. They're the versatile weekender, though not to be worn with a suit.

With their thick rubbery sole they can provide a little protection from the jolts of life and ensure that you won't slip...

However, don't expect to wear them to the Melbourne Cup with your favourite little black cocktail dress!

The Thong

This man is no nonsense. Often found in coastal areas, his joy is in the living. Very relaxed and easy going, he has no great expectations of you – just that you're comfortable and enjoying life.

Not usually a great financial prospect, this man can be a little afraid of hard work. Potentially, they just don't care what others think.

Committed to family and freedom they do not necessarily see the need for financial success.

Let's face it – thongs are summer wear. They go well with your shorts, your summer frocks, even jeans – but come a cold, hard winter and they just won't cut it!

Even the invention of toe socks can't aid the thong's comfort in winter – it just adds bulk that never feels comfortable.

Many of us remember the favourite pair of thongs from our youth. Even the modern versions with 'bling' are still just seasonal attire – not fit for long term use.

The Spanish Espadrille

This guy is suave, classy and charming. If a little on the short side.

Bright and cheery, this guy appears to be lots of fun, but don't underestimate his need for a woman just like his Mama!

Smooth talking, full of confidence and exuding sexuality from every olive skinned pore, this man knows how to sweet talk you. He loves life, food and his Mama. You will only do well if she likes you too.

In reality, a good Spanish espadrille is hard to come by. There are multiple Chinese mock-offs out there without the same long-lasting quality about them!

Patterned or brightly coloured, they are cheery and perk up any outfit. They are Summer attire, and not designed to withstand all weather conditions.

Walking in an espadrille can be quite challenging to the novice. No matter how good you think you look in them, they're chunky and make you walk like a man.

The Motorcycle Boot

We've all fantasised about having a pair of these – even if it was only briefly. They appear particularly desirable when life has thrown you a rough path to navigate. They're tough! In these boots, you think you can walk anywhere.

Not necessarily the prettiest to look at, this man is down to earth and functional. He's a bit of a daredevil who likes to take chances. Despite how they present themselves to the world, these guys are not overly confident, so he won't wear his heart on his sleeve.

If he is interested in you, you'd never really know it. He's the guy sitting across the room at the bar, just looking at you. You will likely need to make the first move.

Let's remember girls – this is a specific purpose boot. It may appear at certain times in your life that the durability of them would make them essential. However, usually once you're through the 'rough patch' and you're looking for some comfort – the hardness of them becomes a harsh reality that you just don't need!

If you live in the bush or you ride a motorbike yourself – then these may be the ones for you. However, they are usually too tough for most.

The Ugg Boot

This guy is the ultimate in comfort – I know women who have kept their Ugg boots around for years... Even when they are badly stained and have holes worn through them!

Soft and comfortable these men are often a little dishevelled. They make you feel warm and toasty and are a fabulous accompaniment to your PJ's,. Especially, on the lounge, when it's raining and cold outside and you want to play 'couch potato' watching movies.

Despite Pamela Anderson's best attempts at making them fashionable – they don't look any good with normal clothes. They should not be worn in public!

Uggies are great – we all love them. They need to only surface in the winter when you're at home alone, a great match for your dressing gown.

Certainly, they have longevity... Most people keep theirs hanging around for years. Be warned – they should not be mistaken for all weather footwear!

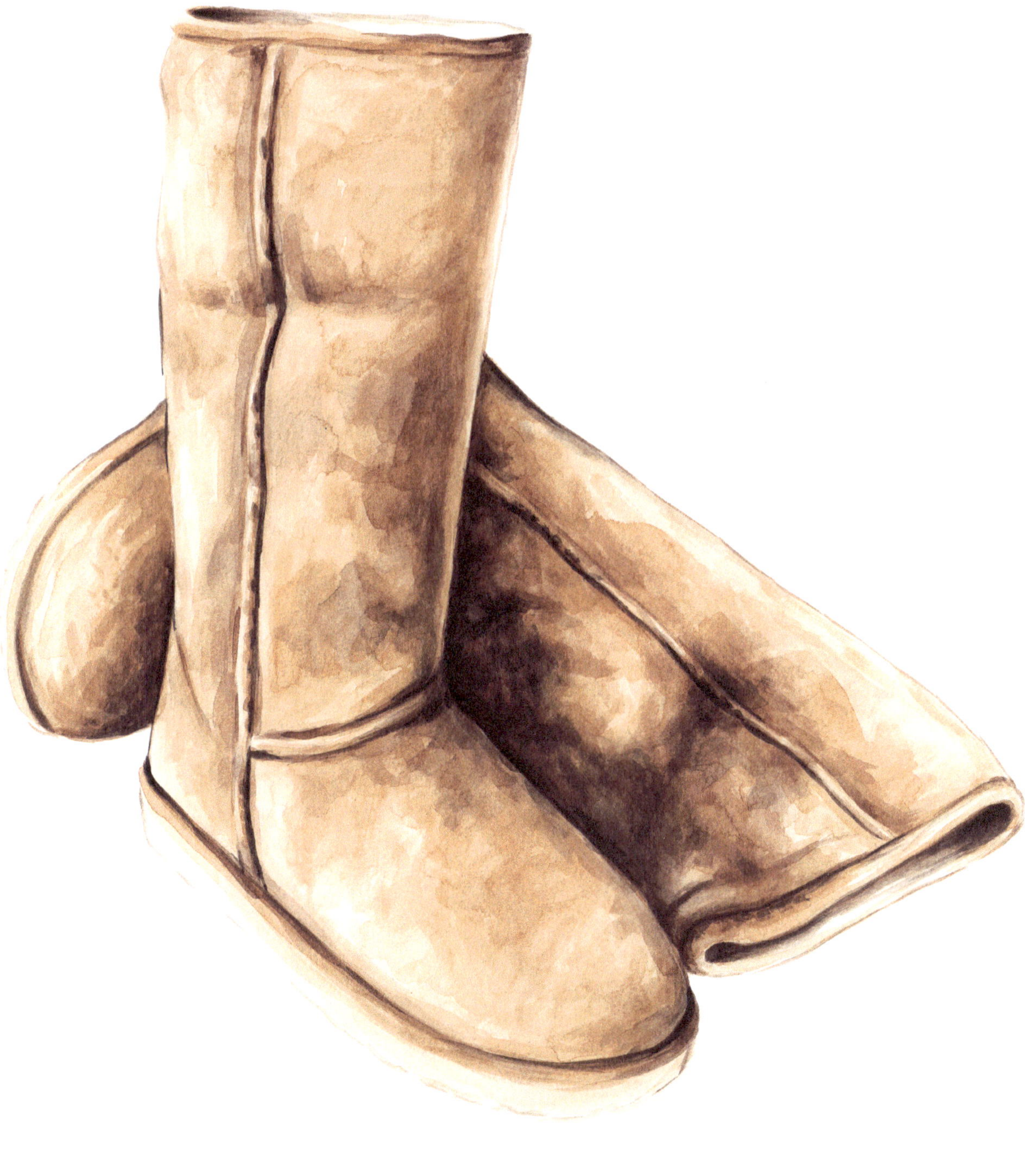

The Ballet Flat

This man is extremely practical and he will slide into your life with seeming ease.

Not too dressy – the Ballet Flat is extremely comfortable to wear and have around. Surprisingly, they can also dress up an outfit almost as well as a 'heel' could do, but without the discomfort.

This man is often the product of a private school education... You know, slightly polished with just a hint of arrogance, they like the finer things in life and they also love their rugby!

It's hard to find fault with the Ballet Flat – they're practical, attractive and suit most purposes. As a fashionista you will love their functionality! Ballet Flats try hard to be beautiful while pretending to be practical.

Truthfully though – they don't provide much support in the long term, and continuous wear is likely to result in unsightly varicose veins and lower back problems.

Although they're perceived as an 'all-weather' shoe, they don't provide much protection. Let's not forget you often get stones in them, causing pain that makes you limp.

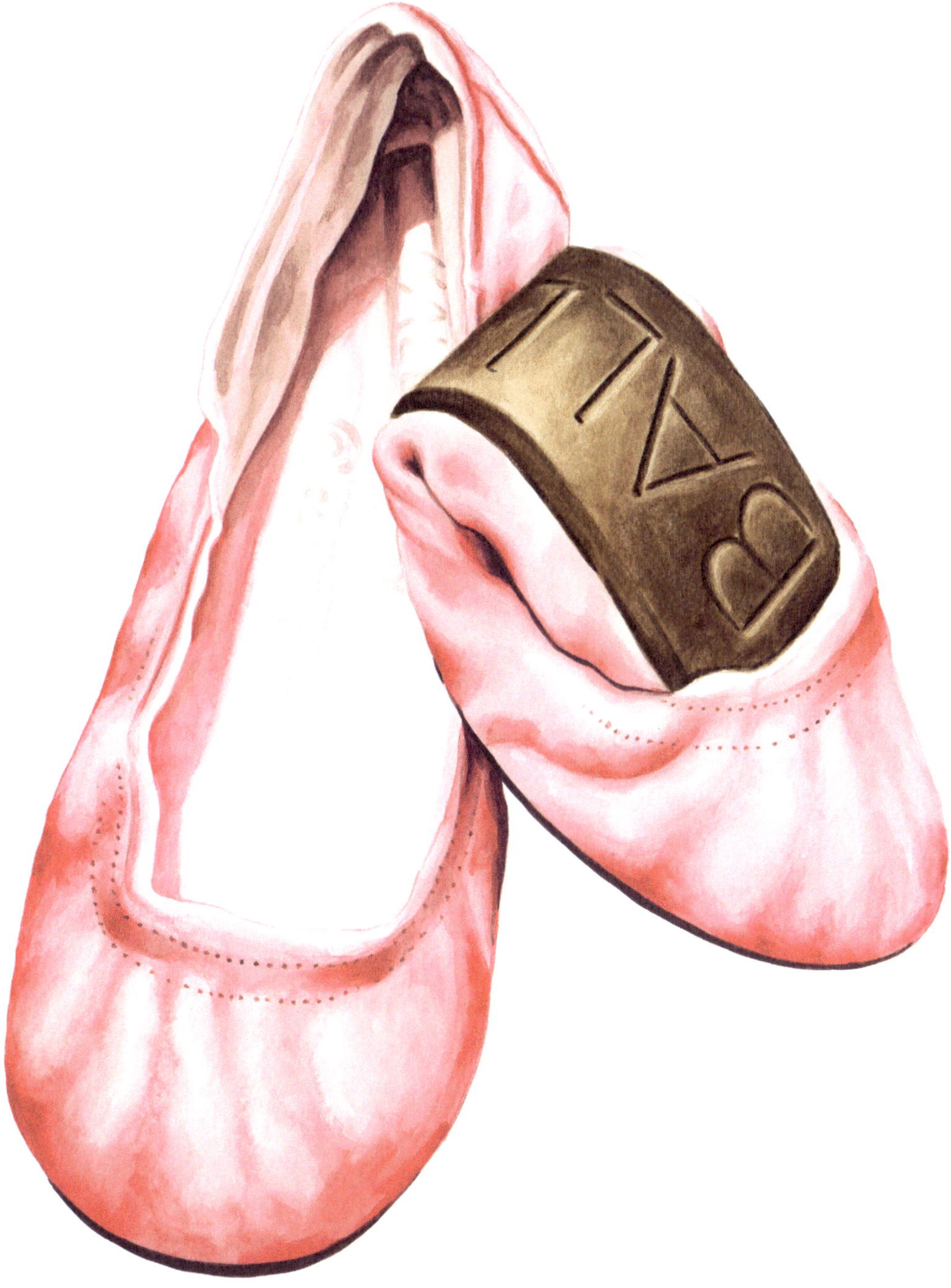

The Doc Marten's

Extremely practical, sturdy and strong – these boots will literally last you a lifetime!

With strength and their traditional styling, these boots have a timeless fashion about them. One that results from their sturdy construction and the use of quality materials.

They can seemingly be worn with anything, and are often teamed with a summer frock for a funky 'alternative' look. But don't be thinking they will match your briefcase!

These guys are often marching to the beat of their own drum. They have a set purpose in life, they know what it is and nothing will dissuade them from it.

Traditional in their views, if this is the man for you then don't plan on having a career of your own – you'll have to follow him wherever the world takes him and be happy to do so.

Doc's can be a fabulous, functional, long-wearing boot – but don't be fooled into believing that there is room in your wardrobe for anything else!

The Court Shoe

The ultimate in 'no-nonsense' footwear, this shoe is practical, comfortable, stable and blends well with whatever you are wearing.

Primarily designed for wearing to the office, or church on Sundays, the Court Shoe is simple, functional and easy to wear.

You may already have several pairs in your wardrobe, the style never really changes but the colour and cut may alter a little with the seasons.

The introduction of shoe bling has given us the opportunity to breathe some life into the old Court Shoe – but don't be mistaken. All that glitters is not a diamond, and 'shoe bling' has a habit of falling off!

A Court Shoe may entertain a bit of shoe bling but it is only ever temporary! This man is stable, no nonsense, comfortable and will probably be a good long-term companion. However, you may find there is no real passion in life for anything much.

Solid, dependable, comfortable.

Ho Hum!

The Birkenstock

Often of European descent or private school extraction, this man is socially aware, environmentally conscious and is often embarrassed about his 'middle class' upbringing.

If you are keen to spend your life eating organic veggies, sending your kids to Steiner School and donating time and money to Greenpeace, then this is the guy for you.

The Birkenstock is the ultimate in engineered footwear. Extremely comfortable and supportive to wear, they mould to your feet and support you well while you walk. They are fully adjustable, everyone should be able to find a comfortable fit here.

When they first hit the European market they were often coupled with overalls and socks – they had a very distinct cultural role and following... Modern Birkenstocks come in a variety of styles – choose from a variety of funky patterns or patent leather.

The message here – if you find a man that is the ultimate in comfort and support but he looks a bit boring on the outside... Don't wear overalls!

Buy him a new wardrobe and dress him up a bit.

The Sandal

Ahhh Summer! The Sandal is potentially the most versatile summer shoe. The variety of sandal styles is seemingly endless.

Each new spring brings new designs with a plethora of heels and accessories like buckles, laces, elastic straps – and colours. The most important thing to remember about wearing sandals is – get a Pedicure!

These guys are your 'average Joes' - the ones who are fun to go to lunch with, but they don't really have any great spark or pizzazz! They are so average that they don't really stand out from the crowd. When dating these guys, you need to be well presented – casual is fine, but neat and clean is a must!

Socks and sandals just DON'T look good – no matter what your Grandma told you... Nor open toes and stockings! 'Peep toes' are for 'peeping your toes' – they don't call them 'Peep Nylons' – do they?

Comfortable and casual is the key to a long-term relationship with this guy. Many sandals can provide good support into your old age... However, it is highly unlikely that only one pair of sandals could last you your whole life.

The Croc

This seemingly indestructible and versatile shoe is a useful accessory. These guys are simple, straightforward and appear to mould to your very needs. They slip on easily and feel instantly comfortable as they flex and form around you.

Crocs are made from recycled materials. They come in an enormous variety of colours and have seemingly endless uses. You can even buy decorative buttons to dress up the most boring looking pair.

But girls, let's be honest... It only takes one or two outings for the shine to wear off a Croc. They never really look good – no matter how casually you are attired. It is also difficult to get the 'genuine article' these days and there are so many 'mock-offs' on the market.

Their very flexible nature results in initial comfort, these guys really give you the sense that you are the centre of their world – their reason for being. However, you soon realise that there is little substance to be found here!

Over time the tread wears down and they lose their shape, to the point that they always slip off as you walk in them. Truthfully, not a lifetime footwear choice...

For The Boys

WHY WOMEN ARE LIKE ALCOHOL...

You can have a rich, full bodied, smooth 40 year old Bordeaux
with hints of raspberry flavours and a soft finish

OR

You can have Passion Pop!

Gents – the choice is yours, but a word of warning.

You can thoroughly indulge yourself in your favourite drink – even to the point of excess and not feel much more than the need to consume lots of water...

However, if you are out being the man about town, living it up, mixing your drinks. Not only do you get very messy, feel very confused and become quite ill – but you'll also discover...

It has cost you LOTS of money.

About Kerry Howard

Kerry Howard, Ms Pink Herself, is a best-selling author, divorcee and single mother of two daughters, she is also a sister and a daughter – she developed the humorous "Why Men Are Like Shoes" as an analogy to explain the concept of dating to her youngest daughter when Kerry started dating again, following her divorce.

It is an irreverent look at dating for women, using an analogy that most women understand – a love of 'shoes'. Kerry is passionate about helping people to experience their best life, even when they are not sure it is possible, and that includes having fun with dating and relationships.

Kerry is a psychologist, executive coach and a self-confessed 'definitive diva'. Kerry has worked with 500+ clients to improve their sense of self, find their joy in life and improve their relationships.

Kerry is also a charismatic keynote presenter. She draws on her own life experiences to deliver powerful messages in a truly authentic way.

Kerry presents on a diverse range of topics including relationships, personal growth and life transformation.

Kerry has an absolute love of being able to assist people to turn their lives around.

"I get pure joy from being able to give somebody a different perspective of themselves and see them make significant change and truly believe it. It's wonderful to see that light bulb moment in their eyes, when they finally understand why they've been doing the same thing over and over and over again and why they don't have to do it anymore! It's awesome when an individual can start seeing themselves in a completely different way, really like who they are, and change their lives as a result."

Put simply, Ms Pink Herself provides profoundly simple, yet humorous insights that are changing the way thousands of women think about their relationships and their lives.

mspinkherself.com

www.ingramcontent.com/pod-product-compliance
Ingram Content Group UK Ltd.
Pitfield, Milton Keynes, MK11 3LW, UK
UKHW061031310726
14089UKWH00009B/190
* 9 7 8 0 9 9 5 4 2 5 1 0 1 *